Contents

Series Title 2
Discipline: Accounting 2
    Topic: Depreciation 2
Author Background 3
Definition of Depreciation 4
Current and Fixed Assets 5
Depreciation Methods 7
Depreciation Calculations 10
Worked Task #1 11
    Solution ~ Worked Task #1 12
Worked Task #2 13
    Solution ~ Worked Task #2 14
Depreciation Schedule 17
Practise Task #1 18
    Solution ~ Practise Task #1 19
Practise Task #2 20
    Solution ~ Practice Task #2 21
Practise Task #3 22
    Solution ~ Practise Task #3 23
Book Value & Salvage Value 26
Selling or Disposing of Fixed Assets 27
Practise Task #4 29
    Solution ~ Practise Task #4 30
Practise Task #5 31
    Solution ~ Practise Task #5 32
Teach a Topic Titles ~ Accounting 33
Further Teach a Topic Disciplines 34

Series Title

Discipline: Accounting

Topic: Depreciation

- Want to get straight to the topic?
- Want material 'lesson ready' or 'student ready'?
- Teach a Topic does just that.
- This book covers Depreciation and follows this format:
    - Introductory theory
    - Worked tasks
    - Solutions to worked tasks
    - Template to calculate depreciation
    - Practise tasks
    - Solutions to practise tasks
    - Dealing with assets taken off the books
    - Practise tasks
    - Solution to practise tasks

All you need for a two or three hour lesson on this topic.

Author Background

I am a trained teacher and have a Master's degree, diplomas in computing and belong to the Institute of Management. I have been a teacher/lecturer for the past 30 years: firstly nine years at secondary level then for the past 21 years at tertiary institutions teaching to graduate level. Over these many years I have purchased hundreds of technical texts. What I have found though is (apart from a couple of texts), I was probably only 'pulling out' one or two areas of information from each book and they have then just sat on my study shelves.

About five years ago, I finally decided there had to be a different way to approach each of my lessons. This is when I created topic booklets. Each booklet represents all that I need for a two hour teaching session: theory, worked tasks, practical tasks and solutions and a review of the lesson. Occasionally of course, dependent on the needs of the students, there might be a need to have another session on a topic – but again, I could use the same format but with additional practical tasks.

These topic booklets are my teaching plan/my guide – but of course it is equally important on how it is presented in front of the students. If the material is there and you are comfortable with it, then you are relaxed in front of the students. Dependent upon the discipline or topic, I still use PowerPoint and other interactive resources.

It is my intention to make life easier for teachers/tutors. If there is a topic that you would like covered; I would welcome suggestions and it would be my pleasure to create a topic book for you (so long as it was within my expertise of course).

Quite importantly, if you find errors in my work; or do not understand my rationale behind a concept – I would be most grateful if you drew that to my attention. Note: For introductory concept teaching in this discipline, I have omitted sales tax (VAT or GST); as I feel there is sufficient learning with new concepts before introducing the 'applied' aspects.

I have taken great care not to infringe on other people's work; although it is hard not to pick up ideas and to develop from those ideas. Likewise, there is so much generic material that I have found repeated in a number of different publications. The amount of help that in recent years is made available on the Internet is a credit to the generosity of the people who provide it (both written ideas, tutorials, YouTube) and again, I have gained knowledge from these sources. However, if anyone feels that my theory or task storylines are too similar to their own – then please let me know and I will alter my material accordingly. I have purchased my own graphics software (IMSI) but occasionally also use free graphics from Google. Any drawings or cartoon strips are my own.

What I have found is that a self-contained lesson topic is what is needed – and that is why and how I have developed my 'lesson plans'.

I hope that you find these topic books helpful.

Contact Details:

Judith Pope
teachatopic@gmail.com

© J Pope 2017

Definition of Depreciation

The process of allocating (or spreading) the cost of a fixed asset over its useful life.

Financial Reporting Standards covering the accounting for tangible fixed assets defines depreciation as follows:

"the wearing out, using up, or other reduction in the useful economic life of a tangible fixed asset whether arising from use, defluxion of time or obsolescence through either changes in technology or demand for goods and services produced by the asset".

A portion of the benefits of the fixed asset will be used up or consumed in each accounting period of its life in order to generate revenue.

By accepting that the life of a fixed asset is limited, the accounts of a business need to recognise the benefits of the fixed asset as it is "consumed" over several years. The consumption of a fixed asset is referred to as depreciation. In essence, depreciation involves allocating the cost of the fixed asset (less any residual value) over its useful life.

To calculate profit for a period, it is necessary to match expenses with the revenues they help earn.

In determining the expenses for a period, it is therefore important to include an amount to represent the consumption of fixed assets during that period ie depreciation. The depreciation expense is shown generally as an administrative expense in the Income Statement.

The provision for depreciation is shown in the Balance Sheet as a deduction from the historical cost of the non-current Asset. The provision for depreciation account is also called accumulated depreciation. Accumulated depreciation is a "contra" account – takes away from the asset account.

Example:

Machinery purchased for $12,000. If the amount to be depreciated is $2,900 the following is the effect of the depreciation on both the Income Statement and the Balance Sheet.

Year 1				
Income Statement (extract)	$	**Balance Sheet** (extract)		$
Administrative Expenses		**Non current Assets**		
depreciation – machinery	2,900	Machinery	12,000	
		less accumulated depreciation	2,900	
				9,100

Year 2				
Income Statement (extract)	$	**Balance Sheet** (extract)		$
Administrative Expenses		Non current Assets		
depreciation – machinery	2,900	machinery	12,000	
		less accumulated depreciation	5,800	
				6,200

Current and Fixed Assets

Depreciation

An important distinction is made in accounting between 'current assets' and 'fixed assets'.

Depreciation represents one of the costs of owning a fixed asset.

'Depreciation' and 'amortisation' are two words describing a similar accounting process:
- depreciation is normally applied to physical assets (trucks, buildings, computers)
- amortisation is used in conjunction with non-physical assets (patents, goodwill, leases)

There are several factors reducing the useful life of an asset. The main ones are:
- physical deterioration (wear and tear)
- obsolescence (becoming outdated)

Two important points to be aware of:
- Depreciation is a non-cash expense.
- The depreciation process does not provide cash for an asset's replacement.

The purpose of providing for depreciation is simply to allocate the cost of the asset over its life. That's it! To replace an asset, what is needed – is to save up!

Depreciation is an allocation of the cost of a fixed asset over its useful life. It is not a valuation process. This is important because depreciation is often taken to mean a fall in value. Although fixed assets are subject to changes in market values, accountants are not concerned with recognising these changes in the financial statements. Fixed assets are acquired for use, not for sale. Therefore the market value is not relevant (except when revaluing an asset).

In order to comply with the matching concept, it is necessary to release a portion of this cost of owning a fixed asset to each accounting period to which it accrues benefits to the entity.

Current assets are those that form part of the circulating capital of a business. They are replaced frequently or converted into cash during the course of trading. The most common current assets are: cash, debtors and stock.

Compare current assets with fixed assets. A fixed asset is an asset of a business intended for continuing use, rather than a short-term, temporary asset such as stock. Fixed assets are those that have been acquired with the intention of keeping them long term for use in the production or supply of goods and services or for administrative purposes. From other perspective – they are assets that yield benefits to an organisation over more than one accounting period.

Capital expenditure is defined as unexpired costs which are expected to provide benefits to the entity in future accounting periods. In other words, while the expenditure on the item has occurred, the benefits of that expenditure accrue to multiple accounting periods.

Important to recognise that the cost of a fixed asset ie capital expenditure includes:
- acquisition cost
- all costs incurred in obtaining the fixed asset eg freight, custom duty

- installation
- all initial repairs undertaken when the asset is first purchased to make it operational

However, all subsequent repairs and maintenance are treated as revenue expenditure.

Fixed assets lose value over time (depreciate). Depreciation is the writing off of the cost of a fixed asset over its useful life. This loss in value may be set by/the result of:
- use: the asset wears out or its uneconomic to repair
- time: the asset becomes obsolete because of technological change or market changes
- legal factors: there is a statutory or contractual life that runs out eg commercial fire extinguisher
- public requirements eg an airline may be required to reduce the noise level of their aircraft – therefore need to replace their planes more regularly, even **though the existing fleet is commercially sound.**

At the end of this life there may be some recoverable value as second-hand goods or scrap. This is called the residual value. The difference between cost and residual value is the amount that will expire and that must be written off as depreciation over the useful life; the technical term for it is the depreciable amount.

The amount that has not been written off at the end of any period is the carrying value traditionally known as book value or written down value. It is important to recognise in reading a Balance Sheet that this carrying value is not a valuation of the current worth of the asset, but simply an unexpired cost.

Note:
- Not every fixed asset will lose value. For example it is very rare for land to lose value.
- Depreciable assets always have a limited life.

The benefits that a business obtains from a fixed asset extend over several years. For example, a company may use the same piece of production machinery for many years, whereas a company-owned salesperson's vehicle probably has a shorter life.

Depreciation Methods

It is necessary to establish a basis for reducing in each accounting period, the value to the entity of the fixed assets; and recognising that decline in value as an operating expense. Because we have to account for depreciation before the asset expires, estimates are necessary.

The following factors are important in the process of measuring depreciation:
- cost of the asset
- ascertaining the useful life of the asset
- determine/estimate the residual amount - in many cases this may be nothing
- with machinery – expected life in units of the asset eg 500 000 photocopies from a machine
- select an appropriate depreciation basis/method for spreading the amount over the useful life
- Inland Revenue depreciation rates

So how much of this depreciable amount is charged against profits in each accounting period? A variety of depreciation methods are available. What is required is to allocate, in a systematic way; and one that reflects (matches) the pattern of benefits derived from that asset an amount to be depreciated between each accounting period of the asset's useful economic life.

Method 1 – Straight-line Depreciation

Assumes reasonably consistent benefits are derived by each accounting period and writes the total depreciation off in equal instalments.

- The straight-line method of depreciation is widely used.
- Simple to calculate.
- It is based on the principle that each accounting period of the asset's life should bear an equal amount of depreciation ie allocate an equal amount
- Constant rate where usage will not vary from period to period.
- Applied to buildings, fittings, furniture.

$$\text{Depreciation} = \frac{\text{cost of the asset} - \text{residual value of the asset}}{\text{useful economic life of the asset (in years)}}$$

Method 2 – Diminishing Value/Reducing Balance

For certain fixed assets, the benefits derived may be high in the early years ie the assets are much more efficient when they are new; but may decline as the asset ages. For such assets, the reducing balance method of depreciation would be appropriate in so far as it matches the depreciation expense with the pattern of benefits.

The diminishing value method of depreciation provides a high annual depreciation charge in the early years of an asset's life but the annual depreciation charge reduces progressively as the asset ages. Progressively smaller instalments each year based on the assumption that services form the asset diminishes steadily throughout the asset's life.

The depreciation is calculated as a percentage of the reducing balance (the written-down or book value) of the asset.

Note: For diminishing value method of depreciation, there is no reduction for perceived salvage value of an asset at the end of its useful life. That is, depreciation in the first year is based on the full cost of the asset.

Method 3 – Units of Output/Use Method

- Based on actual usage of the asset.
- Appropriate where the output of the asset varies from period to period and where it is intended to dispose of the asset once it has reached its estimated usage.
- Applied in businesses that produce/manufacture eg photocopying service, widget manufacturer.
- To apply this method we need to calculate a rate of depreciation per unit of usage:

$$\frac{\text{depreciable amount ie cost} - \text{residual value}}{\text{estimated usage}} \times \text{usage for the particular year}$$

Example: Estimated that a photocopier valued at $20,000 would be used for 3,000,000 copies.

$$\frac{\$20,000}{3,000,000} = .0067 \text{ cents per copy}$$

Apply this rate to the actual usage to find the cost allocation for each year.

eg	2016 year	510,000 copies * .0067 cents	=	$3,417
	2017 year	400,000 copies * .0067 cents	=	$2,680

Method 4 – Sum of Years' Digits (SYD) Method

Like the reducing balance method, this method also results in a decreasing depreciation charge of over the asset's useful life ie the SYD method allocates a large portion of the asset 's cost to the early years of its useful life.

- depreciation rate used in the calculation is a fraction
- the denominator (bottom figure) of the fraction is constant – it is determined by adding the years in the asset's useful life eg where useful life is 4 years it is 10 (1 + 2 +3 + 4)
- the numerator (top figure) of the fraction is the number of year's remaining in the asset's useful life at the beginning of the period

Example: Machinery – cost $33,000, residual value - $3,000, life – 4 years

Year	Depreciable Value $	Rate	Depreciation Expense $	Ending Book Value $
				33,000
1	30,000	4/10	12,000	21,000
2	30,000	3/10	9,000	12,000
3	30,000	2/10	6,000	6,000
4	30,000	1/10	3,000	3,000

In the above example, the calculation of the fraction's denominator was easy. The calculation for assets with a long useful life can become tedious. Can use the following formula instead:

S = N(N+1)/2
S = sum of the years' digits
N = number of year in the asset's life

The sum of the years' digits for an asset with a 15 year life is:

S = N(N+1)/2
  = 15(15 + 1)/2
  = 120

Which Method Should Be Used?

Need to present a financial picture of a business that is a true and fair view of the operations for the period under review. Should select a method of allocation that corresponds to the expected way in which the assets usefulness to the business (its service potential) diminishes.

Once a method of allocation has been chosen, for the sake of consistency, it needs to be adhered to. This does not mean that a change can never be made. If a new method will give a fairer allocation of the depreciable amount, then a change in method can be made but these changes, the justification for them and the effects of the change on profit and asset values must be fully disclosed in order to keep decision makers fully informed when interpreting the accounts.

Notes:

It is important for each business to hold an Asset Register. This might seem a bit involved, but is actually very straightforward. All that is needed, is to list the fixed asset; cost (less sales tax); date purchased; any identifying details eg machine number, chassis number; where asset is located. When the asset is disposed of – that would also be entered. The format of this Asset Register is purely up to the business to decide.

For this workbook, I have am not covering:
- Amortisation (of intangible assets such as goodwill)
- Revaluations

As these are more at the applied financial accounting level.

Further Notes:

It is necessary to check on the rulings of Inland Revenue of your particular country regarding:
- How many months you can claim depreciation for if for example you purchase a fixed asset two months into the financial year. Can you claim for 10 months, can you claim for a full year since it was in the first half of the year – important to be clear on this by going to the Inland Revenue.
- For most countries, it is usual that depreciation for a fixed asset is not claimed in the financial year in which it was disposed of. That is why companies might wish to discard their fixed assets the 'day after' the previous financial year in order to claim the depreciation expense for that year.

Depreciation Calculations

The following is an example of the difference between two different depreciation methods (both of which would usually be allowed by the Inland Revenue:
- straight line
- diminishing value

For the example here – a computer, it would be more usual to select diminishing value. The reason: because computers wear out quicker at the start of their life, they become obsolete very quickly in this technological age or even become unfashionable.

Computer
Purchase date: 1 April 2013

Year ending 31 March	Opening value	Depreciation rate	Depreciation for year	Closing value	Business use	Claim as tax deduction
2014	12000.00	30% SL	3600.00	8400.00	100%	3600.00
2015	8400.00	30% SL	3600.00	4800.00	100%	3600.00
2016	4800.00	30% SL	3600.00	1200.00	100%	3600.00
2017	1200.00	30% SL	1200.00	0.00	100%	1200.00

Computer
Purchase date: 1 April 2013

Year ending 31 March	Opening value	Depreciation rate	Depreciation for year	Closing value	Business use	Claim as tax deduction
2014	12000.00	40% DV	4800.00	7200.00	100%	4800.00
2015	7200.00	40% DV	2880.00	4320.00	100%	2880.00
2016	4320.00	40% DV	1728.00	2592.00	100%	1728.00
2017	2592.00	40% DV	1036.80	1555.20	100%	1036.80

Notice that with the diminishing value method, the larger the expense claim in the initial years compared to the consistent straight line method.

Worked Task #1

Alice Smith buys a taxi for $16,000 in April 2012. Does that mean she writes off the $16,000 in March 2013? No. Because it is going to last her several years.

How much of the cost of the taxi is an expense relating to 2013?

Alice expects the taxi will last six years, and at the end of that time she estimates that she will get $4,000 for it. So we need to spread the net cost (original price of $16,000 less the disposal value of $4,000) of $12,000 over the estimated number of years of use – six years.

$$\frac{\text{Original Cost} - \text{Disposal Cost (Value)}}{\text{Expected Life (in years)}}$$

$$\frac{16{,}000 - 4{,}000}{6} = \frac{12{,}000}{6} = \$2{,}000$$

$2,000 is the amount we must treat as an expense in Alice's books for the year ended 31 March 2013, and the same amount in each of the following five years. This $2,000 is called depreciation.

We call Expenses "expired costs" – something that has been used up. Depreciation is an example of an expired cost ie that part of the initial cost of an asset that has been written off.

Each year's depreciation is also added to that of the year before to find the accumulated depreciation or the provision for depreciation.

Alice's taxi is obviously an asset, but it is gradually being used up. What we must determine is:
- how much of the taxi has been "used up" for the current year – which is shown in the Income Statement and
- how much of the asset is still of value to the business ie the book value or the unexpired cost – which is shown in the Balance Sheet.

Solution ~ Worked Task #1

Alice Smith
Income Statement
for the year ended 31 March 2013

	$	$
Revenue		
Fares		20,000
Less Expenses		
Depreciation	2,000	
Other Expenses	8,000	10,000
Net Profit		**$10,000**

Alice Smith
Balance Sheet
as at 31 March 2013

	$	$	$
Owners Equity			
Capital 1/4/2012		12,000	
plus Profit		10,000	22,000
This is represented by:			
Assets			
Bank		12,000	
Taxi (at cost)	16,000		
less Accumulated Depreciation	2,000	14,000	
		26,000	
Less Liabilities			
Loan		4,000	$22,000

We know that with double entry accounts, EVERY transaction affects at least two accounts. Depreciation is no exception. The method used above to calculate the depreciation is known as the Straight Line or Fixed Instalment method. This is seen as the most suitable for general application. There are a number of different methods available for the allocation of the depreciation. It is important however to check with your own country's Inland Revenue guidelines/rulings on which method to use for particular assets. (For this workbook I will use the New Zealand Inland Revenue guidelines).

Worked Task #2

To find out how much of the historical cost of a fixed asset is to be depreciated, we have to first establish if we expect there to be any residual value ie what we expect to get when the asset is sold. Where there is not expected to be a residual value, the entire historical cost is depreciated.

1. In the following, work out the amount to be depreciated:

Item	Historical Cost	Expected Residual Value	Amount to be Depreciated
Buildings	200,000	50,000	
Motor Vehicles	30,000	10,000	
Fixtures and Fittings	100,000	0	
Plant and Machinery	90,000	10,000	

2. In this task we will use the Straight Line depreciation amount to work out the amount to be depreciated each year. Instead of a percentage allocated, we will work out the amount to be depreciated by dividing the amount to be depreciated by the number of years of expected useful life of the asset ie how long the firm expects to have that asset.

Item	Total Amount to be Depreciated	Number of Years	Each Year's Depreciation Amount
Buildings	150,000	30	
Motor Vehicles	20,000	10	
Fixtures and Fittings	100,000	15	
Plant and Machinery	80,000	10	

3. Each year an expense ledger called "Depreciation" is opened when Balance Day adjustments are being made. This account is **debited** with the annual depreciation for each fixed asset. The contra entry for each debit entry is a **credit** entry in a liability ledger, of which there is one for each fixed asset – this is called Provision for Depreciation or Accumulated Depreciation. These accounts show each year's depreciation for that particular fixed asset and the new total each year.

    The depreciation account appears in the Income Statement while the Accumulated Depreciation account appears in the Balance Sheet.

    Show the Income Statement and the Balance Sheet extracts over the first four years from the following details:
    - vehicles are at $35,000 cost and plant at $80,000 cost
    - depreciation for vehicles is over five years with no residual value and depreciation for plant is over ten years with an expected residual value of $10,000
    - for both – divide by the number of useful years (do not need a percentage to be applied)

4. A car hire firm may decide that the loss of value of their vehicles is highest in the first few years of the vehicle and therefore decides to depreciate using the diminishing value method. Show the first three years accumulated depreciation for a vehicle that cost $40,000 and is to be depreciated at 40% per annum.

Solution ~ Worked Task #2

Task 1

In the following, work out the amount to be depreciated:

Item	Historical Cost	Expected Residual Value	Amount to be Depreciated
Buildings	200,000	50,000	150,000
Motor Vehicles	30,000	10,000	20,000
Fixtures and Fittings	100,000	0	100,000
Plant and Machinery	90,000	10,000	80,000

Task 2

In this task we will use the Straight Line depreciation amount to work out the amount to be depreciated each year. Instead of a percentage allocated, we will work out the amount to be depreciated by dividing the amount to be depreciated by the number of years of expected useful life of the asset ie how long the firm expects to have that asset.

Item	Total Amount to be Depreciated	Number of Years	Each Year's Depreciation Amount
Buildings	150,000	30	5,000
Motor Vehicles	20,000	10	2,000
Fixtures and Fittings	100,000	15	6,667
Plant and Machinery	80,000	10	8,000

Task 3

The depreciation account appears in the Income Statement while the Accumulated Depreciation account appears in the Balance Sheet. Show the Income Statement and the Balance Sheet extracts over the first four years from the following details:
- vehicles are at $35,000 cost and plant at $80,000 cost
- depreciation for vehicles is over five years with no residual value and depreciation for plant is over ten years with an expected residual value of $10,000
- for both – divide by the number of useful years (do not need a percentage to be applied)

Item	Value	Life	Residual Value	Depreciation
Vehicle	35,000	5	0	7,000
Plant	80,000	10	10,000	7,000

Income Statement
Expenses
Administration
depreciation - vehicle   7,000
depreciation - plant   7,000   14,000

Year 1
Balance Sheet
Non current Assets

vehicle	35,000		
less accumulated depreciation	7,000	28,000	
plant	80,000		
less accumulated depreciation	7,000	73,000	101,000

Year 2
Balance Sheet
Non current Assets

vehicle	35,000		
less accumulated depreciation	14,000	21,000	
plant	80,000		
less accumulated depreciation	14,000	66,000	87,000

Year 3
Balance Sheet
Non current Assets

vehicle	35,000		
less accumulated depreciation	21,000	14,000	
plant	80,000		
less accumulated depreciation	21,000	59,000	73,000

Year 4
Balance Sheet
Non current Assets

vehicle	35,000		
less accumulated depreciation	28,000	7,000	
plant	80,000		
less accumulated depreciation	28,000	52,000	59,000

Task 4

A car hire firm may decide that the loss of value of their vehicles is highest in the first few years of the vehicle and therefore decides to depreciate using the diminishing value method. Show the first three years accumulated depreciation for a vehicle that cost $40,000 and is to be depreciated at 40% per annum.

Vehicle

	Cost Price	DV %
	40,000	40%

Year 1
Balance Sheet
Non current Asset
vehicle		40,000	
less accumulated depreciation		16,000	24,000

Year 2
Balance Sheet
Non current Asset
vehicle		40,000	
less accumulated depreciation		25,600	14,400

Year 3
Balance Sheet
Non current Asset
vehicle		40,000	
less accumulated depreciation		31,360	8,640

Depreciation Schedule

This layout may assist you in keeping a record of depreciation. Use a spreadsheet to assist in the calculations. There is no 'right' layout – it has to best suit you for ease of use and viewing.

Depreciation Schedule

Asset Item:					
Depreciation Method:					
Calculation:		Cost:	Life:	Residual Value:	Rate:
Year		Opening Book Value	Depreciation Expense	Accumulated Depreciation (end)	Closing Book Value
	1				
	2				
	3				

Asset Item:					
Depreciation Method:					
Calculation:		Cost:	Life:	Residual Value:	Rate:
Year		Opening Book Value	Depreciation Expense	Accumulated Depreciation (end)	Closing Book Value
	1				
	2				
	3				

Asset Item:					
Depreciation Method:					
Calculation:		Cost:	Life:	Residual Value:	Rate:
Year		Opening Book Value	Depreciation Expense	Accumulated Depreciation (end)	Closing Book Value
	1				
	2				
	3				

Asset Item:					
Depreciation Method:					
Calculation:		Cost:	Life:	Residual Value:	Rate:
Year		Opening Book Value	Depreciation Expense	Accumulated Depreciation (end)	Closing Book Value
	1				
	2				
	3				

Practise Task #1

Polly's Popping Popcorn

Polly Bowman decided on a career change; where she could be outside meeting the public more. On 1 April 2003, she purchased a popcorn producing machine for $16,000. The machine was expected to give service for 10,000 hours of production time after which it would be scrapped. For the years ended 31/3/2016 and 31/3/2017 actual usage was 2,800 and 3,600 hours respectively.

1   Answer the following questions to determine the depreciation using units of use:
    a   What is the economic life of this machine?
    b   What is the residual value of the machine?
    c   What is the depreciable amount of the machine?
    d   Using the units of use method of allocating cost, what is the rate of depreciation?
    e   How much depreciation will be written off in each of the two years?
    f   Show how the machine will appear in the Statement of Financial Position at 31 March 2017(extract only).

2   Assume the machine was expected to give service for five years. How much depreciation will be provided each year if the straight-line method of allocating cost was used?

3   Assume the machine was to be depreciated at a rate of 20% per annum diminishing value, following the maximum rate allowable for taxation purposes. Calculate the amount of depreciation for the years ended 31/3/2016 and 31/3/2017.

4   Lizzie's business made a profit of $86,000 in the year ended 31/3/2017 before providing for depreciation. Calculate the final net profit for the year under each of the depreciation methods previously used ie:
    a   units of use
    b   straight-line
    c   diminishing value

Solution ~ Practise Task #1

Polly's Popping Popcorn

Question 1

a) economic life: 10,000 production hours

b) residual value: nil

c) depreciable amount: $16,000

d) rate of depreciation:
    depreciable amount $16,000
    units of use   10,000
              = $1.60 per production hour

e) depreciation amount for year ended:

    31/03/2016   2,800 hours x 1.60   = $4,480
    31/03/2017   3,600 hours x 1.60   = $5,760

f) Balance Sheet as at 31/3/2017:
    (extract)   **Non Current Assets**
                        popcorn machine   16,000
                        less accumulated depreciation 10,240   5,760

Question 2

Annual depreciation amount using straight line method: $3,200

Question 3

Diminishing value method.

Depreciation amount for year ended:
31/3/2016 -   20% x $16,000   = $3,200
31/03/2017 -   20% x $12,800   = $2,560

Question 4

	Units of Use	Straight Line	Diminishing Value
Profit before depreciation	86,000	86,000	86,000
Depreciation	5,760	3,200	2,560
Profit	**80,240**	**82,800**	**83,440**

The highest profit is reported under the diminishing value method. This will not always be the case.
In years of very low usage, the units of use method would probably result in a higher profit.
In this case the DV rate is not cosnistent with the five year economic life under the S-L method.
If the economic life used as the basis of the DV was the same as for S_L (and it should be) then profit would be higher under a straight line method.

Practise Task #2

Peter Plummett ~ Plumber

Peter needs you to calculate the depreciation for the financial year ended 31 March 2017.

Below are the details of his fixed assets purchased on 1 April 2014 (when he commenced business). Also shown is the book value as at 1 April 216.

Description	Depreciation Method	Cost	Closing Book Value
general plant	10% DV	$21,000	$17,010
fixtures and fittings	20% DV	$15,000	$9,600
vehicle #1	35% DV	$20,000	$8,450

The following fixed assets were purchased during the financial year:

Description	Purchased	Cost
machinery	1 May 2016	$32,500
trailer	1 July 2016	$4,000
plant & equipment	1 October 2016	$11,000
vehicle #2	1 January 2017	$23,000

The depreciation method for all new items is diminishing value: machinery – 40%; trailer – 7%; plant & equipment – 25%. Vehicle #2 is same as vehicle #1.

Task 1
Write up the depreciation schedule for all of the assets. Include the accumulated depreciation for the assets that you have the book value for. Do your own calculations to check that the figures given you are correct.

Task 2
Create a new depreciation schedule for 31 March 2017 that includes all of the assets. You will need to calculate the depreciation for the new assets based on the number of months since they were purchased.

> For example, an asset costing $12,000 purchased on 1 October 2016 could only claim 6 months of depreciation. $12,000 * 20% = $240/12 * 6 = $120.

Task 3
Vehicle #1 was sold on 1 June 2017 for $18,000. Write up the general journal entry for the disposal of this asset.

> For Task 3, refer to page 28 for guidance on how to deal with the disposal of a fixed asset.

Solution ~ Practice Task #2

Peter Plummet ~ Plumber

Task 1

Date Purchased	Asset	Cost	Depreciation Method	Depreciation %	Depreciation	Accumulated Depreciation	Book Value 1 April 2016
1-Apr-14	General Plant	21,000	DV	10%		3,990	17,010
	Fixtures and Fittings	15,000	DV	20%		5,400	9,600
	Vehicle #1	20,000	DV	35%		11,500	8,450
1-May-16	Machinery	32,500	DV	40%			
1-Jul-16	Trailer	4,000	DV	7%			
1-Oct-16	Plant & Equipment	11,000	DV	25%			
1-Jan-17	Vehicle #2	23,000	DV	35%			

Task 2

Date Purchased	Asset	Cost	Depreciation Method	Depreciation %	Depreciation	Accumulated Depreciation	Book Value 1 April 2017
1-Apr-14	General Plant	21,000	DV	10%	1,701	5,691	15,309
	Fixtures and Fittings	15,000	DV	20%	1,920	7,320	7,680
	Vehicle #1	20,000	DV	35%	2,958	14,458	5,543
1-May-16	Machinery	32,500	DV	40%	11,917	11,917	20,583
1-Jul-16	Trailer	4,000	DV	7%	210	210	3,790
1-Oct-16	Plant & Equipment	11,000	DV	25%	1,375	1,375	9,625
1-Jan-17	Vehicle #2	23,000	DV	35%	2,013	2,013	20,988

Explanation: machinery depreciation based on 11 months.
trailer depreciation based on 9 months.
plant & equipment depreciation based on 6 months.
vehicle depreciation based on 3 months.

Task 3
General Journal
Vehicle #1

Date	Details	dr	cr
1-Jun-17	accumulated depreciation	14,458	
	bank	18,000	
	vehicle #1		20,000
	gain on sale		12,458
	Being the disposal of Vehicle #1		

Practise Task #3

Regent Cinema

David Favell wants you to set up a depreciation schedule for the assets of the cinema. Below is an extract (not all figures are provided) from Regent Cinema Theatre's trial balance:

projectors	18,000	bank overdraft	4,000
seating	31,000	long term loan	11,000
premises	100,000	capital	129,310
petty cash	100	creditor	5,500
cash	1,000	accumulated depreciation –	
fixtures and fittings	12,400	fixtures and fittings	
		seating	
		projectors	
		premises	

Straight line method for depreciation is to be used for:
- seating – residual value is estimated at $5,000 after 5 years of depreciation
- fixtures and fittings – residual value is estimated at $5,000 after 10 years of depreciation
- premises – residual value is estimated at $55,000 after 20 years of depreciation

Diminishing value method of depreciation is to be used for:
- projectors at 25% per annum on cost

1. Draw up a five year schedule of depreciation for the assets.

2. Explain why the diminishing value method of depreciation has been chosen for the projectors.

3. Write up a separate Balance Sheet for each of the first three years. Only the Fixed Asset extract section is required.

Solution ~ Practise Task #3

Regent Cinema
Trial Balance

	dr $		cr $
projectors	18,000	bank overdraft	4,000
seating	31,000	long term loan	11,000
premises	100,000	capital	129,310
petty cash	100	creditor	5,500
cash	1,000	acc depreciation - f&f	740
fixtures and fittings	12,400	acc depreciation - seating	5,200
		acc depreciation - premises	2,250
		acc depreciation - projectors	4,500
	$162,500		**$162,500**

Regent Cinema
Balance Sheet as at 31 March 2003

	$	$	$
Proprietorship			
Opening Capital			$129,310
This is represented by:			
Current Assets			
petty cash	100		
bank	1,000	1,100	
Current Liabilities			
bank overdraft	4,000		
creditors	5,500	9,500	
Working Capital			(8,400)
plus Non-Current Assets			
Fixed Assets			
projectors	18,000		
less accumulated depreciation	4,500	13,500	
seating	31,000		
less accumulated depreciation	5,200	25,800	
fixtures and fittings	12,400		
less accumulated depreciation	740	11,660	
premises	100,000		
less accumulated depreciation	2,250	97,750	
		148,710	
less Long Term Liabilities			
long term loan		11,000	137,710
			$129,310
Year 2			
Fixed Assets			
projectors	18,000		
less accumulated depreciation	7,875	10,125	
seating	31,000		
less accumulated depreciation	10,400	20,600	
fixtures and fittings	12,400		
less accumulated depreciation	1,480	10,920	
premises	100,000		
less accumulated depreciation	4,500	95,500	
		137,145	
Year 3			
Fixed Assets			
projectors	18,000		
less accumulated depreciation	10,406	7,594	
seating	31,000		
less accumulated depreciation	15,600	15,400	
fixtures and fittings	12,400		
less accumulated depreciation	2,220	10,180	
premises	100,000		
less accumulated depreciation	6,750	93,250	
		126,424	

Regent Cinema

Depreciation Schedule

	Method	Cost $	Years	Rate	Residual Value $	Amount $	Year 1	Book Value	Year 2	Book Value	Year 3	Book Value
Fixtures and Fittings	Straight Line	12,400	10		5,000.00	740.00	740.00	11,660.00	1,480.00	10,920.00	2,220.00	10,180.00
Seating	Straight Line	31,000	5		5,000.00	5,200.00	5,200.00	25,800.00	10,400.00	20,600.00	15,600.00	15,400.00
Premises	Straight Line	100,000	20		55,000.00	2,250.00	2,250.00	97,750.00	4,500.00	95,500.00	6,750.00	93,250.00
Projectors	Diminishing Value	18,000		25%			4,500	13,500	7,875	10,125	10,406	7,594

Book Value & Salvage Value

Book value is the difference between the cost of an asset, and the related accumulated depreciation for that asset.

Book Value = Cost - Accumulated Depreciation
Book Value = ($12,000 - $10,000) = $2,000

The company will stop depreciating the truck after the end of the fifth year. The truck cost $12,000, but only $10,000 in depreciation expense was taken. The remaining book value is equivalent to the salvage value established when the vehicle was purchased. Book value will be used to calculate any gain or loss when the truck is sold or traded.

Depreciation expense spreads the cost of major equipment and assets over a period of time that spans a number of years.
Amortization is used to allocate the cost of intangible assets, such as patents, copyrights, trademarks, and franchises.
Depletion is used to record the cost of natural resources extracted from the earth.

There are three main events in the life of any asset:
- acquisition
- useful life
- disposal or retirement

Depreciation is referred to as **cost recovery**. The government allows you to use the cost of plant assets to offset income. You recover your cost a little bit at a time, over a number of years. Each year you reduce your income tax expense, by an amount relative to the cost recovery amount for that year. It's a slightly strange concept if you're not involved in preparing income taxes. But it does make sense if you think about it a bit.

For financial statement purposes, depreciation reflects a number of different influences that each affect an asset over its useful life.
- recognise physical deterioration
- recognise obsolescence
- recognise a reduction in market value
- recognise benefits derived from using the asset
- apply a logical, systematic cost allocation over a relevant period of time
- apply the matching principle

Each of these is important to a company. When assets are purchased, the cost is reflected in the Balance Sheet. Depreciation expense transfers that cost to the Income Statement in order to reflect the effect of the items listed above, in the financial statements.

Selling or Disposing of Fixed Assets

After selling or disposing of fixed assets, **the company no longer has the asset**. This requires a journal entry to remove everything in the accounting records relating to the asset.

The depreciable cost and accumulated depreciation relating to the asset must both be removed, or reversed. There might be a gain or loss when disposing of assets. A journal entry records the disposal. Let's assume on September 1, the ledger shows these balances for a piece of equipment.

General Ledger

Equipment

Date	Description	Debit	Credit	Balance
Sep-1	Balance	$7,000		$7,000

Equipment – Accumulated Depreciation

Date	Description	Debit	Credit	Balance
Sep-1	Balance		$5,600	$5,600

With the ledger detail above we will add the additional information to reflect different examples.

General Journal

Date	Account	Debit	Credit
Sep-15	Accumulated Depreciation	$5,600	
	Equipment		$7,000
	To record disposal of equipment		

The journal entry is now in balance. The steps to take to achieve this:
- Write up what you already know – the original cost of the equipment and the accumulated depreciation. They will be on the opposite sides than when they were first entered.
- Leave two lines blank of the journal entry – to record the sales price and gain or loss.

Equipment Sold for a Gain

If equipment is sold for more than its book value there will be a **gain**. Gains are recorded with credit entry (similar to revenue). If the equipment is sold on September 15 for $2,000. The gain will be:

Selling Price	$2,000
Less: Book Value	($1,400)
Gain	$600

Date	Account	Debit	Credit
Sep-15	Accumulated Depreciation	$5,600	
	Bank	$2,000	
	Gain on Sale		$600
	Equipment		$7,000
	To record disposal of equipment		

Equipment Sold for a Loss

If equipment is sold for less than its book value there will be a **loss**. Losses are like an expense and recorded with a debit entry. If the equipment is sold on September 15 for $1,000. The loss will be:

Selling Price	$1,000
Less: Book Value	($1,400)
Loss	($ 400)

General Journal

Date	Account	Debit	Credit
Sep-15	Accumulated Depreciation	$5,600	
	Bank	$1,000	
	Loss on disposal of equipment	$ 400	
	Equipment		$7,000
	To record disposal of equipment		

Equipment sold for a Wash

If the equipment is sold equal to its book value there will be a **wash**. In this case there is no gain or loss is recorded. The equipment is simply removed from the books. If the equipment is sold on September 15 for $1,400.

Selling Price	$1,400
Less: Book Value	($1,400)
Wash	$ 0

General Journal

Date	Account	Debit	Credit
Sep-15	Accumulated Depreciation	$5,600	
	Cash	$1,400	
	Equipment		$7,000
	To record disposal of equipment		

Equipment Junked

If the equipment is junked there will be a loss equal to its book value. We call this **abandonment**. The item is usually just dumped, sometimes with associated dumping costs. Incidental costs are revenue expenditures, and are not included in calculating the capital gain or loss.

Selling Price	$ 0
Less: Book Value	($1,400)
Loss	($ 1,400)

General Journal

Date	Account	Debit	Credit
Sep-15	Accumulated Depreciation	$5,600	
	Loss on abandonment of equipment	$1,400	
	Equipment		$7,000
	To record abandonment of equipment.		

Practise Task #4

Fast Print Ltd, which has a 31 March balance date, purchased a printing machine for $450,000 (GST% exclusive) on 1 April 2013.

Depreciation was calculated using a 33% DV rate.

On 31 January 2018 the machine had become so outdated that it had to be sold. Only received 11,000 for it.

Required

Task 1

Calculate depreciation on the printing machine for the time that it was owned ie for the financial years 2014 – 2017.

Task 2

Write up the appropriate expense section of the Income Statement for the financial years 2014 – 2017.

Task 3

Write up the Fixed Asset section of the Balance Sheet for the printing machine for each of these years, calculating the accumulated depreciation and the book value.

Task 4

Write up the general journal entry for the disposal of the printing machine.

Task 5

What effect will the loss on disposal have on Fast Print Ltd's net surplus for the year ended 31 March 2018?

Solution ~ Practise Task #4

Fast Print Ltd

Task 1

Year	Asset	Depreciation Method	Cost	Depreciation	Accumulated Depreciation	Book Value
2014	Printing Machine	DV 33%	450,000	148,500	148,500	301,500
2015				99,495	247,995	202,005
2016				66,662	314,657	135,343
2017				44,663	359,320	90,680

Task 2

Income Statement

2014 *Administration Expenses*
    depreciation   148,500

2015 *Administration Expenses*
    depreciation   99,495

2016 *Administration Expenses*
    depreciation   66,662

2017 *Administration Expenses*
    depreciation   44,663

Task 3

Balance Sheet

Fixed Assets
    printing machine   450,000
    accumulated depreciation   148,500   301,500

Fixed Assets
    printing machine   450,000
    accumulated depreciation   247,995   202,005

Fixed Assets
    printing machine   450,000
    accumulated depreciation   314,657   135,343

Fixed Assets
    printing machine   450,000
    accumulated depreciation   359,320   90,680

Task 4
General Journal

Printing Machine

31-Jan-18		dr	cr
	accumulated depreciation	359,320	
	printing machine		450,000
	bank	11,000	
	loss on sale	79,680	
	Being the disposal of printing machine.		

Task 5

The net surplus for the year ended 31 March 2018 will be decreased by the loss on disposal which will be shown as an expense. Usually this will be shown as Other Expenses; not included in Operating Expenses.

Practise Task #5

 I Care Optometrists

I Care Optometrists has a 31 March balance date. The business purchased a new eye testing machine on 1 April 2013. The machine cost $77,000 (GST exclusive), and additional costs were $3,000 (GST exclusive). The machine has an estimated useful life of 10 years and a residual value of $12,000. Unsure which depreciation method to use, the accountant (you) will compare SL at 25% and DV at 18%.

Task 1
Set out the details as given above.

Task 2
Calculate the depreciation for the financial years 2014 – 2016 using the straight-line method.

Task 3
Calculate the depreciation for the financial years 2014 – 2016 using the diminishing value method.

Task 4
Show the Balance Sheet extract for the asset for the 2016 year.

Task 5
The optometrist sold the eye testing machine on 17 June 2016 for $50,000.

Calculate the loss or gain on sale. Assume depreciation has been calculated using the diminishing value method.

Show this as a general journal entry.

Solution ~ Practise Task #5

I Care Optometrists

Eye Testing Machine

Task 1
Asset Cost:

eye tesing machine	77,000		
additional installation costs	3,000	80,000	

Machine Life:
   10 years

Residual Value:
   $12,000

Depreciation Method:
   straight line   25%

Depreciation based on:
   80,000 - 12,000   =   68,000

Task 2

Date	Asset	Cost	Depreciation	Accumulated Depreciation	Book Value
2014	Eye Testing Machine	80,000	17,000	17,000	63,000
2015			17,000	34,000	46,000
2016			17,000	51,000	29,000

Task 3
Depreciation Method:
   diminishing value   18%

Depreciation based on:
   80,000   no residual value involved with DV.

Date	Asset	Cost	Depreciation	Accumulated Depreciation	Book Value
2014	Eye Testing Machine	80,000	14,400	14,400	65,600
2015			11,808	26,208	53,792
2016			9,683	35,891	44,109

Task 4

Balance Sheet (extract)
Fixed Assets

eye testing machine	80,000	
less accumulated depreciat	35,891	44,109

Task 5

General Journal
Eye Testing Machine

Date		dr	cr
17-Jun-17	accumulated depreciation	35,891	
	eye testing machine		80,000
	bank	50,000	
	gain on sale		5,891
	Being the disposal of asset.		

Teach a Topic Titles ~ Accounting

- Accounting Equation

- Perpetual versus Periodic Inventory

- Income Statement (and Trading Statement)

- Balance Sheet

- Terminology and Concepts

- Depreciation

- Statement of Cash Flows

- Partnerships

- Interpretation and Analysis

- Breakeven Analysis

- Budgeting

Further Teach a Topic Disciplines

- Accounting Practices
- Business Communication
- Business Computing – Intermediate
- Business Computing – Applied
- Financial Accounting
- Management
- Marketing

www.ingramcontent.com/pod-product-compliance
Lightning Source LLC
Chambersburg PA
CBHW041300180526
45172CB00003B/911